Morning Lit:
portals after Alia

Omar Sabbagh

Cinnamon Press
:: small miracles from distinctive voices ::

Published by Cinnamon Press www.cinnamonpress.com
The right of Omar Sabbagh to be identified as author of this work has been
asserted by him in accordance with the Copyright, Designs and Patent Act,
1988. © 2021, Omar Sabbagh.
ISBN 978-1-78864-127-2
British Library Cataloguing in Publication Data. A CIP record for this book
can be obtained from the British Library.
Designed and typeset in Bodoni by Cinnamon Press. Cover design by Adam
Craig © Adam Craig.
Cinnamon Press is represented by Inpress.

Acknowledgements

The author would like to thank the editors of the following journals,
magazines, anthologies in which many of these poems, or earlier
versions of such have appeared previously: *Agenda* ('Fatherhood', 'The
Beach') and *Agenda Online* ('*You Convince Yourself*', 'Portrait Of A
Man'), *Acumen* ('A Daughter', 'Coup d'état', 'Waiting For Alia', 'The
Sacrifice', 'Sleep'), *Envoi* ('On Digging', 'Heartbeat'), *Indelible* ('The
Book Between Morning And Morning', 'The Lay Of The Land', 'A
Hunger Artist', 'Chocolate Gifts', 'A Glass Of Water', 'Education'),
Interlitq ('The Diary Of A "Loser"'), *(T&F) New Writing* ('80 in the
Frame'), *Two Thirds North 21* ('No Two People'), *Finito World* ('More'),
Telos Magazine ('The Crows', 'Good Advice', 'A Teetering Place'), *New
Humanist* ('Broken Thought'), *The Beltway Poetry Quarterly* ('The
Manichee', 'Sunlight Upon Sunlight'), *The Best Asian Poetry 2021*
('Where Does A Man Go?', 'Matter Beyond Matter', 'The Specialist'),
the *New England Review* ('Letter To An Innocent In A Time Of War',
'Unhomely'), *Nexus: The International Henry Miller Journal*
('Lawrence Durrell') and *Exeter College Register* ('Twenty Years In The
Making'). There are also a very few poems, appearing formerly in my
2020 collection, *But It Was an Important Failure*, republished here for
apposite reasons.
Permissions to quote from *Justine* by Lawrence Durrell and from Philip
Larkin's 'Home is so Sad' courtesy of Faber & Faber Ltd. Permission to
quote from 'All Right' in *The Selected Poems of R S Thomas* courtesy of
Penguin.

Contents

Epilogues 115

For Faten
Between the rock and the hard place
We find a home

"'Still, one has the illusion of freedom; therefore don't be, like me, without the memory of that illusion. I was either, at the right time, too stupid or too intelligent to have it; I don't quite know which... The right time is *any* time that one is still so lucky as to have. You've plenty; that's the great thing; you're, as I say, damn you, so happily and hatefully young. Don't at any rate miss things out of stupidity... Do what you like so long as you don't make *my* mistake. For it was a mistake. Live!'"

Henry James, *The Ambassadors*

'It was as if the whole city had crashed about my ears; I walked about in it aimlessly as survivors must walk about the streets of their native city after an earthquake, amazed to find out how much that was familiar had changed. I felt in some curious way deafened and remember nothing more except that much later I ran into Pursewarden and Pombal in a bar, and that the former recited some lines from the old poet's famous "The City" which struck me with new force – as if the poetry had been newly minted: though I knew them well. And when Pombal said: "You are abstracted this evening. What is the matter?" I felt like answering him in the words of the dying Amr: "I feel as if heaven lay close upon the earth and I between them both, breathing through the eye of a needle."'

Lawrence Durrell, *Justine*

'Our souls, shame-wounded by our sins, cling to us yet more, a woman to her lover clinging, the more the more.'

James Joyce, *Ulysses*

Morning Lit

‘

Author's Notes

You Convince Yourself

'You tell yourself: I'll be gone
To some other land, some other sea,
To a city lovelier far than this
Could have been or hoped to be...'
          CP Cavafy, 'The City'

You convince yourself
you'll find a different planet
spinning on a different axis
each time. So, you underplay the kiss
given you, and the terror that
you cannot shield
because a world is just that, a matt
abyss, the terror that
comes brimming like liquor quick
to poison, tar, the envy of the stone, bricks
that make no home; that terror that
you convince yourself
will never tally, never find a home –

well, my friend, aren't they
the brittle arrows
you've always parried,
you've always known?

Crap Decisions

an autobiography

He looked to the left, he looked to the right, he looked ahead, he looked behind, and all he saw was detritus, rejected members like dead and broken leaves, broken spines to boot which had failed even to bite the treading feet that had crushed them. They lay strewn across a path that was, in its fullest sense, a finished path. They lay strewn like aborted poems, whose first phonemes had predicted it all, the inborn stilled and stilted flavor, the trite lilt, the twee, the rigorous lack of any real or compelling conception, inkling, divination – all of it: the resplendent way it had always been destined to bound and bound and bound towards its immolation, and a fatal bind. He was shackled from the start, perhaps, but cuffed himself further by going farther than his own presiding self-awareness – as just outlined. He'd always wished to title his autobiography: *Second Chances and Seconds*. But even that gambit had died.

A Teetering Place

Where do I go, driven by this erring beast
Each time, with fathomless feet, my eyes
Somehow closed, and somehow neat –
Where do I go after the true and licit feast?

There is shrieking once more, and from
The balcony I hear the base spirits roar
About this place, a teetering place
By which I dye a dyer's dye, and am

Filled with a drop of good and surreptitious
Grace. A mere dreg or pellet can be the sum
Of that flowing water we then become, fast, slow –
The speed of a stranger's wonderland

Always-already unknown... Where do I
Go, riven by a hounding pack of hounds
In a hirsute bacchanal, while this turning Saturn's sound
Stays, but as a muffled sound? I don't know

Where I go, by this music somehow found
Inside of me. I pressure the dark below
The surface and find this slow, calm ore
Come to adorn the vehicle of something more.

Portals After Alia
an introductory note

The work comprising this volume, comedic, tragic, joyful, angry, playful or deeply-serious, are smallish labors of love. No claim is made to the possible superlative reaches that poetic and more generally creative forms of writing can reach. This work, responsive to the entrance into the world of what is now the total tot and sum of my own world, are portals for the author and his reader which tend towards or within those tender limits that, delimited by one small body, one small bundle of proverbial joy, are limitless. Sometimes a window or a door become more than themselves, can veritably grow wider and longer and seemlier for the seeing eye, by the very frames that make them and restrict them to what they are. By limiting the scope and themes of these creative entries, entrances, to various kinds of paean for a daughter and to the other epiphenomena that accompany for nearly all of us, surely, the new burdens – which are the lightest weights – of parenthood, the hope is that this act of self-limitation may prove to amplify the effects of the overall course of this book: permitting, thus, what has been a deep and wide 'responsiveness' to transform as well into 'responsible' literary work. A poet or creative writer can sometimes produce his worst work where his heart is most engaged or invested. The wrong kind of distance between him and his work can wreck the best intentions, preventing that kind of reflexivity that should be like a bodyguard to successful work, allowing the right choices, selections, decisions. Often enough when one's heart is literally full and overflowing, the enjambments of feeling are too transitively related into the object language of the literary artefact underway. That said, the very invoked notion of a 'portal' suggests I hope that entry, my entries, are indeed truly 'travelling' some kind of transformative distance. Between verse and some happenstance prose, my main, if not sole, intention has been to honor what has to be, now, the full meaning of my life. A deeply self-involved, if not quite purely selfish, man like myself may exhibit to those he loves and who love him a tendency to obtuseness, the kind of empathic blindness that can be endemic to the warp and weft of artistic instincts as they drive and form his workaday behaviour. But the hope beyond hope is that for *this one* beloved, the author, a father, really has no choice in the matter: he is rigged to love unconditionally, unconditioned by the more worldly concerns that betray, with arch desirousness, even an artist's supposed independence. He is, in short, given entrance to a better, larger world, a world which is in fact without limits; and transcendence of a surer pedigree is offered him, pillowed upon a tray, by the creation, in part, of a true and truer life – not by the mere begotten things, scraps, of literature; or at least, the aping at such.

Whether making the reader chuckle, weep, grow plum with fellow-feeling, or what have you, the entries that comprise this book are, at the last, more than all the readers' possible responses: because they are portals after *Alia*. Wherever you, dear reader, may travel to, rest assured: the destination is and will be a good one, rhyme upon rhyme.

Prologues

On Digging

For my father, Mohamad Sabbagh
Dubai

He passed many years ago, now, parked and glossed.
I teach his poems nearly every day. I trust the sparks
Of all his embers still glow, glimmer; I have to.

And through the eddies, the heartening ebb and flow
Of the rug and weave of all this time, textures passed
In the company of the angles of the angel-dark,

I have realised a truth filled with the violin's mark –
You know, the unlucky one, sublime, perhaps, a thorough
One that lasts. The years since have lifted the curse

And I feel better speaking to you now. The rasp
Of all the digging done, now as then, then as now,
Comes up twenty years away – and the effect, filmic

As it ever was. In this sunk, son-bit movie, though,
The emanations revolve; beams turned upwards, they ask.

Where Does A Man Go?

For Mohamad Sabbagh
Beirut

Where does a man go, the distance of his worship
Set in the mold of an ersatz prie-dieu (a buckled body
Bloodless still) when opened towards the gifts
He'd pardon with, nearly wide as lifelong?

Look, for instance, at this large square room
Warmed by a furnace we may call love. Then look
At this drum: it longs for its beat-beat to return from
A supplicant's waylaid prayer, as God, in good time, took.

Where does a man go, beaten now by the lips
Of legions without a care for the kindness a song
May serve, beyond the felled or shattered way
A man goes fallen by? There is no more lift

In the ways he walks, in the avenues of some
Small fraction less than naught. Look, then look
Again: these are the farthest reaches a man can take
Towards a father, or what flesh and blood become.

The Crows

For Mohamad Sabbagh
Dubai

Are these crows or kids, just wandering around
After dark? I've grown used to the sight
Of dozens of crows, schools of black-bodied birds
Soaring or swooping in black formations
And so much so, I hardly notice them anymore.

But now as I notice them, the gawky sounds
Of the dark in the dark voice of the night,
I wonder awhile, searching my hoard of words
For what I'd like to say to them. They might listen,
And perhaps I'm placed to offer them a door,

Offer them more than their own dark heights?
Are these crows or kids? It's hard to tell: I can't
Quite make them out, not enough to be sure.
And yet, here in the desert, gripped by this desert chill,
The darkness, the darkness I've known of old

Grows touched a touch, stony, stale. I've heard
The beating heart in their darkling call, decades
And more, and know it to be what it is: a small helplessness –
Just that. I look back from the window, by the desk,
And see a picture of my father. His placid smile

Seeks for nothing there: he seems complete
In this picture, quieted, calm, wrapped in total peace.
And so, when I turn my mind again, turn
And pleat my thoughts around the question:
I realize I've nothing to answer for here.

There aren't quite words for the rotten wish
Of these shrieking birds, busied by the rot inside
Of them. And I was a sky and host for these
Years before they entered the earth. I was their height
Back then, as I am now their height and once again.

1. Deliverances

An Agreement

Fetching, like an incoming, livid sea,
She approached the infinity
Of puckered sand: and all of me.
And she had free white lips
With which I couldn't help
But agree, and agree, and agree.

Heartbeat

Clutch and release, grasp, clinch and let-go
In a small part of this curving parcel of life,
Black and thorough in the frame of the machine

Needling an eye through the seamless pouring
Of love twined by two – I sing my first and my
Final song, a lyric I hear on a harp without strings.

All my nightmares have led to the dream of you;
All the lived, the viscid horrors, turn at the beauty
Of one who cannot be anything as yet, but true

As nightfall and sunrise, the light at its seam,
The bright corner where all things are enough, this choir
Of one violin, and a drum and a pea-small sound

Like the gabbling of gold from a golden halo. Half-
Moon, beloved nut – never was anything so round
As you, strolling down the leaf-strewn avenue of

This daft and singular cleverness, your mother's
And mine: the womb of your sturdiest ground, the bard
Quick to lose his tune, poor before the price of words.

Fatherhood

For Alia Sabbagh

It happens into life, of course, but very slowly.
The same tongue that, pacing, lodges words
Into the grooves they were made for, the very same

Seams itself in the lipless kiss you find
You name your being with, now a father, now
An awning shading smiling flowers by the sea...

And all the worst, and all the thickest losses
That may've robbed your sum of time here
Are gluts now-glutted, now-stoppered, stopped;

It was a lottery you won the whole year round
The one day she birthed – and with a lightness of touch
That proved your pen a maker

Of naught but awry, off, gauche and clanging sounds...
Fatherhood is like a tree, cut, then found again
The same in the self-same forest: green is aghast

With white, as they mix in this the freshest sap of things.
And I think I'll take a twig with me, too, for truth, a souvenir.
And I think this girl, my girl, is now my only, final fear.

A Daughter

For Faten

The wild cry of this undulant night
Whose blue's more silver than purple
Slides like a voice in search of signs
Like words, foils of the brave sublime –
The flesh of many minds like symbols.

I can't find a straight, untethered line
Like this except in her, the unchained sounds
Of my future – the night is white with a girl…

And then I look to my left, to my right,
Seeing things like glossy marbles
Strung to build my rope of time; to lull
The knot that signs at the knotty middle –

Unravelled now by a carrying wife
Whose care holds more than unskinned love.

Coup d'état

For Alia Sabbagh

Deep in this valley, this valley
Like a green and undulant pocket
A small tickle of water stirs
From out of the undergrowth,

Trickling the earth
With its wet promise, a wet
Promise to which the world concurs
Deep in the valleys
Of each.

And you cannot dub what follows
Anything but the far
Richer, greener meaning; and in

The barest, deepest bellows
Of his heart his heart laughs and sings.

Deliverance

A Fiction Of The Fact
For Alia Sabbagh

The day had arrived. As Haitham lugged the final suitcase from the elevator to the door of their fourth-floor flat, his pounding heart and his racing mind seemed both to be on the cusp of bursting out of the straits of his body and onto the small part of world before his feet. Those feet now walked (as though disembodied) with infinite excitement the last few steps before kingdom come. His first child, indeed, the first real true fruit of the otherwise rotten tree of his life, had emerged, entering the world of the living six days previously.

She wasn't expected so soon; and that was why Haitham had been continents away at the moment of her birth, there, in what it might be true to say was his truer homeland, London, England. He'd wrapped up a few necessary odds and ends, and then had snatched the soonest flight home.

And so, there he stood, in his large, puffy, tar-colored duffle-coat, looking like a bushy-haired hobgoblin. He was pressing the doorbell with such persistent, iterative force that a small shard of cracked white paint broke off, falling away to the blue-carpeted floor, a forlorn waif, or like a sacrifice to propitiate the lusty pagan god he just was, standing there, hurried and harried inside and out. The phalanx of flaming pyres inside of him were set off by a new green hope, and if there was anything to lament, anything worthy of solace, it was the dying-away of the old fear that he might not live to see his life – in sum, or across the pained plains of its marred extent – offered its own small way for redress. The scales of his life for the first time in decades felt balanced, their seesaw stilled by a golden child. Here was peace at last; or its prospect at the least. Another white wispy fleck of paint cracked and fell away, just as the front door wound open.

When Melda saw him, standing there, panting away, her wide-lipped smile whispered for him to keep as quiet as possible. The baby was sleeping. Haitham greeted his mother inside as well, and after hugs and kisses and muted exhilarated exaltations, he was pointed in the direction of the sleeping infant, a small bundle of slightly reddened, leavened flesh, wrapped in layers of tope. He approached, gently bending down on one knee, and placed his lips on the forehead of his newborn daughter, and just as he did so, her small mouth widened into a yawn, her slate blue eyes opening in a quick flicker like exotic precious stones. For an infant she'd an abundant head of dark hair, line after line of damp dark threads, which were later to lighten into a full head of chestnut curls and streaks of rich, living straw. Haitham noticed, almost immediately, how proportionally tall she was and was to be, the length of the bundle of newfound life before him evident in that. Her head, like his own, and indeed like both his parents' heads, was also a touch larger than the average, between an oval and a square. When he made these observations in hushed tones of awe, his eyes wide-eyed in shock and fascination, Melda merely said, loosening her clenched palms from their attitude of near-prayer to hold his own:

'She's ours. She's our own beautiful, beautiful baby.'

The rictus she wore seemed to grow out of her olive eyes. It seemed to him that some of their dark and sultry cruelty had transmogrified from acerbity into sweetness, a sweetness he'd rarely clocked in her. Gone, in that moment, the rancor between them, and the bitterness of much acrimony. Gone, too, swept away in a happy tide, the frail stilts or props that had seemed to hold them up as paramours or partners. Gone, the final brittleness of their connection. All that went between them, coded by the presiding silence now, was, for the moment at least, as adamantine as one would wish. Reaching to plant the first kiss he'd given her in over two months, he merely said:

'Well done. Well *done*.'

The baby had fallen back into sleep. Haitham, his mother and Melda retreated to the far end of the living room, seating themselves with a strange and pregnant delicacy on the large sofa at the other end of the room. They spoke in rushed whispers, darting the odd doting look across the way. Life, it seemed to all of them, was just here.

The Princess Gospels,

Or,
Diary of a Newborn
For Faten and Alia Sabbagh

The Art of Shit

Amira shat today – which is great news. It wasn't as prolific a shit as we've come to expect by now, but it was certainly a robust attempt to ape former graces.

Its middling nature adumbrated, let me say however that it was a shit whose khaki-green hue and whose plunging, slushy texture, were so true to us that neither I nor Farah were stirred into any animus or worry beyond the staple relief, tinged as ever with tones of wonderment. Each time, usually three days or more in the making, Amira deigns to proffer us an excretion we are touched, and it's like a small effort at redemption, or a kind of shriving for us; as though our new-born girl's shit made claim to resume the burden of both the batches of her parents' sins. When Amira shits our world totters, on the brink: a Calvary if you will. We await that wetted load of crocodile and brown on preened tenterhooks. In fact, perhaps it's truer to say that it's us, my wife and I, who are the truer new-borns in this luminous scenario: naked, bawling, purple, wet...

The world's our proverbial oyster then – after Amira: our deliverance, due, undue...

The Philosopher's Stone

Somewhere in one of Plato's dramaturgies, the character, Socrates speaks of his own peripatetic discipline (that of philosophy) as in effect a 'preparation for death'. Presumably, that rigorous, questioning, reflective discipline is deemed (and dubbed) as such because both death (or dying) and thinking your way outwards, towards the true(r) essence of whatever part of reality may be at hand – *presumably*, because both involve a healthy kind of alienation, of self-distancing. The root-intuition of the analogy might have been, I'd venture, the inkling that the ego, the principle (and principal) of reflective personhood – that part of the human rigging that supposedly makes us levitate, more leavened, above the rest of the animal kingdom – that it was *precisely this* self-hugging part of human being that rendered us the more dogs-bodies than bodies-of-God. That, in short, the species, *homo sapiens* became saner and sager the more he or she let-go of the self-obsessed tendencies of the very same, selfhood. The less pompous animal is the wiser one; or something along those lines, I'd guess, anyway... *Just so,* Amira's birth (plus the sheeny wax of her incumbent worldly berth) has been very much *like* a dose for us of that same discipline. We live at her beck and call: all ears, eyes, tips, tongues. And perhaps *it is* true in some way that we are closer to being prepared for our own nullity because of our extant princess.

I write these (no doubt erring) observations while my baby sleeps (like a baby) in the travel pram – which is, I now say in my pride, like the souped-up Range Rover of prams, the Bentley, even. Not the faintest whiff of stirring: my girl is a lake (probably Swiss), a swan on that lake, and the crystalline sky above them both. I always know when she is going to stay like this, placid in deep slumber, without a word – or at least, a gargled, garbled sound that might be the former's quickening forerunner, its ace-like avatar. I know when to place her into her regal, fig-coloured vehicle (down from her sleepy dock on my shoulder) because her body goes completely slack, with not the smallest tendon's tension – indicating that the nap is hale, true, lasting, bona fide. When my girl is like that, the most beautiful dead weight, she shows herself indeed to be (and be and be) a truly golden, gilded burden – much more *like* a philosopher's stone than your sundry, garden-variety kind. If we, my wife, myself and the rest of you of the unshriven earth are fleeting tokens of 'Becoming', *well,* let Amira be seen and sensed for what she is – more redolent of 'Being', being in her dwelling if you will.

The Alchemy of the Burp

Once upon a time, she did both simultaneously: burp; fart. It was an awakening from Alpha to Omega; it was instinct with epiphany, realisation – but in the more gaseous mode. However, between the gas down there, the gas back there, and the gas up here, *well,* there is a long, urgent due of difference. Whether Amira farts or not is, in the grand scheme of things, neither here nor there – though always welcome of course. Milk-ridden, though, to see and sense her release a burp – that happening reveals itself: a high priority for rallying, for hearts and minds. It's not just the utility of the burp that presses, compels, not just the fact that without the efficacious burping she will not sleep, unleashing rackets instead; it is also the fact that when Amira burps there is in evidence what can only be called, with awe in tow: a soul-brewed alchemy. The whole of our lives, past, present and to come, brighten, tending now more towards the kind of (now-transfigured) wholeness which is nearly always felt to be (so) absent, or at least, unattainable in our workaday lives. A burp from Amira transforms the constellations, and, thus, our fates – yours, no doubt, too. The gas released is holy. The resulting smile, sacred. Amira, give us more good news!

The Functionary

I awoke to a raucous, shrill demand. Bellowing my name, Farah's voice sounded aflame, roaring with pins. She needed my help, as a waking, woken diversion, to distract our princess while the girl was being changed (diaper and dress-code). Stumbling out of bed, still sleep-ridden, sleep-mounted, I stood there at the corner of the changing table, wagging a small orange dinosaur and telling half-slumberous tales to Amira's astonished gaze, shooting smile. My heart was in it, of course, but I was still half-busied by sleep. It must have been a comical sight, as I stood there, one eye closed, one eye trying to be on the up and up, my hair a wide-spangled fiasco, my words, drooling numbers, and my right hand keeping up the effort to shake the small orange dinosaur whose belly made a rattling sound. I felt like a functionary, hauled in to do menial labour. Or, in a more decorous idiom, like a civil servant to the other two – wife, child – branches of government: namely, judiciary and executive. And it seems to my weary eyes that the revolution, should it ever come (even in the wake of this prolonged metaphor), will not arrive any time soon. Us men: husbands, fathers: we are cattle, more meat than helpmeet – but happy perhaps to be so; and from time immemorial.

Baby Kungfu

What is it to dance? Is it the resultant dance, or is it, as a late romantic trope has it, the dancer in the dance? You see, now at just past seven weeks-old and weighing-in at close to five kg, Amira has grown, developed not just physically but in terms (or in wondrous signs) of alertness, awareness and apprehension; *and by all accounts*, not just ours, her parents': *preternaturally so.* True, I was indeed wearing a bright red shirt, but I could have sworn that when

38

we danced and played, sported, gambolled, Amira began for the first time to make not only reactive moves and noises, but purposive, willed (or chosen, intended) and exploratory ones. She has moved in her inner equilibrium from a practitioner of your staple baby Kungfu (all bent then shooting arms and legs, but styled at times and graceful) to the position (a Kleinian term, I believe) of a baby scientist. For I'm quite close to certain that these new sounds she makes to accompany her rote (meant preciously) movements are indeed like little experiments played-out on the backend of some kind of baby-process of hypothesis-making. Farah and I expected as much, in any event: our doctor during pregnancy couldn't help but wax lyrical about how active and playful Amira was when scanned and pictured in the womb. So, yes: before the flowering, leavening of her intellectual brilliance, she must colour her object-world with dance-moves – which are the former's behavioural equivalent, or simulacrum. One further note, apposite, I pray: I am growing muscles again in my shoulders, arms. As I say, yesterday I and my princess danced to the impassioned yet oaken sounds of the Gypsy Kings, and I was carrying her the whole time, to boot. And I sweated, soliciting by the time I went to bed a goodly, long-lost ache in my feet and body. Newly-born, thus, I hope to resume some kind of form, fitness over the coming, first year of Amira's life; it seems, and thankfully, an easy way to get back into an exercise routine: I've a deep bed of motivation here. While my biceps, deltoids grow more tumescent, I and my baby continue to dance; and sometimes, while Farah is changing her, bad cop, I can't help but delight in my complementary position (a Kleinian term, I believe) of, *well*, good: *or far, far better cop!*

The Saddest Story

There is a look in my daughter's eyes, which are at present of a blue closer to slate-grey, but soon to blossom, I'd guess, into turquoise, opal or emerald; there is a look emitted from those same gazelle-shaped orbs (now circled by a thin ring of tear) which says: INTEGRAL SORROW HERE INHERES, or just: *Hunger Becomes Me* – I can't tell which. Unlike either my syntax or my use of punctuation, there is nothing stagey about her minor bouts of sadness. Amira means 'princess'; and just like one: breeding, unbeknownst breeding, pre-empts any theatrical display. No; she is soulful, but without the mood music – or even any soundtrack at all; what she shows is the mere passion for life, expressing itself, and lighting up her small nursery with that well-known sad story. But it racks at the heart, you know, to see your little one aching with need, not quite sundered into desire as yet (see Laplanche, after Lacan, after Freud), and not to have the breasts filled with the milk which might slake, sate – the wife in the shower, say. The wife wresting a couple of (smuggled) hours of sleep of an afternoon, such privateering being by turns needful; and so on. And when I'm not able to dance the time away with her, I tell Amira tales. The small and orange dinosaur serves at times; and we've now been gifted her second official toy, a sky-blue, pillow-soft bunny-rabbit; but my tales tend to be short and, admittedly, truncated, disquisitions on symbolic logic and other follies. Amira, if I'm interpreting her belches and/or her gurgles aright, seems to side more with the freer school, if not quite the fuzziest. Sometimes we discuss laughter – yes, that too.

Saga of the Cut Cuticle

So. I'm sat there, bunched, slumped, slouched, bevelled at a curving angle against the left side of the sofa. Amira is a bundle of joy and a rugby ball cradled in my arms. After time, legions and rigmaroles, I'm finally about to be released to do my due diligence, a joy. But just when Farah gives me the green light – *at last*, a fin and its chomp – to begin the bottle-feed, she notices a cuticle on my right hand, the feeding one, which has a dash of dried blood on it. The deluge begins. The catastrophe. The universe shrieking in a thimble. There are clowns and bear-tamers scaling the walls of the living room! NO! NO! NO!

Thus, and so: another ten-minute delay. Like the chief of the cabin crew, I inform Amira of the slight delay, due to a smidgeon of dried blood. She bears no grudge of course, but still continues to wail: that is her duty to all babies in the international federation of babes (a surreptitious union. Indeed, to prolong the metaphor: I've not the heart to haul in strike-breakers. I, the capitalist in question, at hand, concede. After all, as many a Marxist political economist will tell you, what you save as a capitalist in labour costs you lose, by the same token, in so far as that same pool of workers needs must constitute the market for your goods, so that an undue saving on the one side saps the force of profit on the other end.) Incidentally, my sister, Amira's own aunt, informs me again and again (she works as a banker of sorts) that communism doesn't work, that it was proven not to do so. I won't argue that now. But I will take a simpler tack: tell me, does capitalism work? Has it ever? Take a look around you. And so on. But where was I? Ah yes, the delay in the supply of milk, given raging demand. (Perhaps here, I should say, your average bourgeois economist is proven wrong. Amira is supplied before she has any actant demand; Farah's breast milk, in a nice counter-intuitive slap in the face, *increases* the more it supplies: it's like an inverted image of what Keynes called a 'liquidity trap.' And so on....)

Anyway, after a year or two of anti-bacterial washing and rinsing I was allowed, at long last, to feed my girl. And she demolished the bottle of milk; the white, silken stuff verily galloped down. But bad tidings boded, thus: the incumbent burps (an ever-sly breed) seemed bound to be stragglers, difficulties, banes. But this is fatherhood...

The Vietcong

Amira had just let-loose a ka-ka far yellower and fairer far than she was wont to (as she ages, her shit brightens); the trouble was that on discovering the stool-passage, lifting her legs, her mother was regaled with a second helping. And then, as though with adult irony, indicating cherries on top, at the start of her diaper-change Amira unleashed a nice fountain or spree of pee. She was clearly enjoying herself. But at the sight (site) of ground zero as it were, with such a wide display of shitty largesse, it behoved us, my wife and I together, to give Amira her infantile bath. The basin prepared with water at medium or medium-rare, we didn't dunk her in toto, no; merely a shuttling movement, in and out, using, I suppose, a kind of guerrilla tactics: which, to prolong the unkempt image, made Amira the American Empire and myself and Farah the Vietcong...

Home-Bound,
Or,
Our Happy Manacles

Of course, our lives are now directed (if not quite guided) by many new markers, such as: the little egg-shaped monitor that registers any room's temperature; the three or four thermometers placed at different access-points across the apartment, the baby's long thin closet which looks like a pregnant column bearing pinks and whites and dovish greys, the green of baby pistachios or mint in a mellow mood, and so on; such as, the phalanxes, again variously-placed across our smallish apartment, of milk bottles sterilised with monkish rigor and clandestineness, the various timbres of antibacterial wipes, stamped by different, rarefied brands, each one with a different jousting style, each one with a different badge of heraldry recorded in the lists; and so on, and so on. It's a joy to be manacled thus; it's as though Marx's theory of commodity fetishism turned its face, and with a deaf ear was granted the boon of a diplomatic mission in a far happier country where all aliens are natives. So, yes, we are reconciled (not resigned) to being: to being home-bound. I miss the opportunity to pose like a rat-packed man over a whiskey the colour of mahogany made to laugh by amber. I miss the license (not freedom, I'd say) to roam and amble, stroll and fritter my time by the hour: now, each half-hour segment of the day has its burden of ironclad duties. I miss the time to commune with God, my odd bout or dose of mystic stupor; because even the Deity takes second place in the wake of our princess. I may well miss many things, but this new regime of binds (not bondage) goes with the territory. We are not trapped here in any way; we are, rather, as we feel: liberated by the cuffs of a new world order.

Fever About Fever

Farah is obsessed, *haunted* by the spectral thought of Amira getting a fever. This, her *idée fixe* 'about' Amira's temperature has us checking it every three and a half minutes. But the sadder thing of it is, the sadder to report, is that she herself has worked herself up into a feverish or waking-hypnagogic state – phantasms and sleepwalkers journeying through her mind. I have enough Latin to know what the 'ablative' is: it's the 'orum' ending, I think; as in: *coincidentia oppositorum* (a term I first spied in Jung). Farah, we might say, is a patient or victim of *feverus feverorum*. There are many accounts of this mild disease in Tacitus (not Livy), I believe – a historian who was contemporary of Christ.

The Lives of Lullabies

When we sing from day to day, not in the infant idiom of sweet garbles, of honeyed gobbledygook, we do our best to be in tune – most of us anyway. However, a very strange thing happens when we begin to sing to our children. The tunes, the songs, *nay, even the tailor-made lullabies*, begin – like characters of a novel in the sleeping mind of a fertile novelist – to show (feral) lives of their own.

I think I've caught myself *at least three times* singing: '*Twinkle-twinkle little star*' to the music — (but not the score of course; I happen to be allergic to staves) — of '*ring-a-ring-a-roses*'...

Being a parent can be a gentle kind of madness: I love therefore I am.

The Music of the Stools

As far as I understand it, there are many creation myths (see Tolkien, for example) that make use of the trope of music, music as the operator into presence, doing the bona fide work of creation. Presumably, of all the media, it is music that is considered the most advertently metaphysical. And of course, it is. I can turn my face and eyes away from a painting, a book; but music, sound, whether tunefully patterned or not, is just there, just there, whether I happen to like it or not. Just so, there is an equal music (Vikram Seth has a novel of this name), but of the stools. This mustard-coloured gunge has its own laws, and they are outlaws, if I may coin a phrase aping wit: the baboon in question not quite as sublime in its formula as the reality it wishes so to monkey (which is to say: words do not suffice in pursuit of these wholegrain melodies).

The Book Between Morning And Morning

For Alia

There is no book like this timeless
between morning and morning.

The day begins again
and again and no more of
the same again with
this girl who travels distances
unravelling gifts
once wrapped in the smithy
of a deep red place that
can't be forged anymore.
No hot lane nor
kiln or pottery and no

pottering about anymore,
none enough to still or stop this
moving name I find again
percolating in pins that mend
and seam so much and

with a svelte type of shock this
cradle sounds
outwards to the roundness of a whole
world founded and known
for a smile
ratcheting the beating ricochets
there. There is no coverless
book like this
and no book ever was ever so coverless

no story or tale or lay
holds
an equal music
quite as resonant as
these sounds in semiosis
craving outwards, upwards
in the vivid sunlight

from out of her crystal
slate-blue eyes. Slowly now but
adamant

I look to the north and find
a different place changed
in the mind echoing within
the same. And the mind
has no weapons
except the heart which might move it so

the apt distance
which is quiet and infinite.

And the mind has no steel
rapture except
by the motor of the heart.

And the laws of my reason now
wake in a graveyard where
felled pride falls
again and again and again.
A girl now speaks

out from the book
of her happiness like no other
book ever.
Its words though its
traveling travelling words

and such invisible
print in such
invisible
print.

Morning Literature

For Alia

As crickets bark their soft glow sound
and the night sky follows
closing in

from the shallows sins
in the lower-case turn
initials without a name
inside the poem.

One man holds a drum.
He beats it with a deuce of sticks
like a pair of loving eyes
because he knows a thing or two
about the night sky.
He knows the way it fits
perfectly,

the deepness of the furrow
in its periwinkle-blue
peppered by an edifice

he knows about.
He knows a bit, a little bit
about this due
to a red fog he's lived, the false
and artificial light
by which he's come to
his deliverance

to barter with
summations
tokens
the talons
of such nights such
nights such
nights.

So
he turns to the dragons of his youth and to
the scale-less-ness
equal, always, to this wide dark-
limbed blue
and offers himself

like a strip of cloth tugged and shadowed
by the wind's small lips this
night with all of its
burdens of sickness and in
health

the final cheering.
That the fear was always wider
than the love that was his compass

but that that has changed.
He can read again within
the far more limpid silky tome

of his heart the wider stronger range
gifted him with a quicker beat
a mind

manumitted and made again
and more

cleansed
and undefiled
by this the
morning literature

of his child

and the night sky is in his hands.

Waiting For Alia

She awakes soon; I've trust. The newly-fathered day
and the inbound dawn, unshackled from the dark
and blue and grey, will come down again to
make the sky – or dice a verb, unheard-of till truth's

toll, tax, *and now*: the grammar of your waking, the quick
language by which you gabble and make your way
through the incoming, humid light, watering the face
of the world with your syllables, lips, a fig-colored breeze –

all of this, these, are as nothing compared to what
I now believe: that you are in fact the richest lore
a man has faith in; more than the wisdom in the cut
and quiet of all the edges, the foregone dogmas

the world knows. A fathered acolyte, I turn in fair
distances of worship, searching the secret of who you are.

The Stumped Anthropologists

For Alia

Each morning before dawn I awake to the splendid niggly sounds of my infant daughter, gabbling about her dreams no doubt and – on those wonderous occasions when my heart soars like an arrow or an eye through mist – betimes garbling the syllables for 'Daddy.' She rises onto all fours, props herself up, wagging her little clever head of almond curls and chestnut waves, and searches the morning, opening curtains, gifting her father yet again a bellyful of manna and divine hope. I alight, a shooting bullet upwards out of bed, and my lips begin to quiver, savoring the approach of the first dawning kiss they will place on those little puffy cheeks whose skin's texture silk and satin in their utmost reaches covet. I know this because I have spoken with both, silk, satin, and both have displayed deep but distinct signs of jealousy, the kind of imprimatur that doesn't quite fit their pedestals as your staple icons of grace. Indeed, when in concourse with these two smooth-billed numbers, they have begun in my presence to rage, pointing fingers, because, I can only assume, Alia Sabbagh has them at an inexorable advantage – doubled now by the roughshod, slipshod tongues they display, from which there is no return, about which there is no salvaging of face. No, these textures, famed for their touched sanctity, turn into devilments, because they just cannot countenance my daughter, Alia. Alia, by turns, gurgles a few daft kindnesses, dispatching them into their told-off places. For Alia is the ambassador of grace, her spirit, one of the few acmes of generosity – the other noble pinnacles being, say, mountaintops in the vicinity of Tibet, or the Dalai Lama himself in his most gifted mood. Alia Sabbagh dyes her world, the truest iris. Those two orbs of slate and blue, which are romantic beyond romanticism, wake to a world in which her father's almonds become white and worshippers. The truth is, it's she who's given me a name, Sabbagh, 'Dyer.' But my words are sots, dead colors, and if they gather any light and life or mirth, it is because they are mere reflections and refractions (sheepish, secondary qualities) derived from the dawn-strong emanations of her sun. Fathers of daughters are so rarely fathered thus; becoming a father for me has been like coming into the inheritance of my childhood again, and with far more intension than your twee or triter sense. Between that halcyon childhood and the birth of Alia, I have been placed in various benighted positions – pariah, scapegoat, outcast, exile, martyr, villain, hero, and so on, the usual litany accompanying your workaday, fatal mix of tragedy, injustice – but with the coming of Alia, razed tablets, cleared slates, blank cheques, blue skies in idioms of whiter.

Giving luck itself its own mint of fortune, Alia has more than one morning in a day. Like most infant children, she naps twice or thrice in the course of her blessed passage between the arcades of sunrise and sunset. And when she awakes noon-time, say, her late morning doze come to a rightful close, and when her eyes speak and her lips emit sounds that see again and again into my blood's own heart, I can only wish her another festive morning. She goes to her feasts. She makes a goodly kaka. Betimes she bathes in the buoyancy of warmed breast-high waters my wife has prepared in her tub which is the color of her eyes. She may nap again towards the end of the afternoon, on the cusp of evening, waking for a final feast or libation, before retiring to her nights. (This is an old trick: laying out the plot in a few bare-knuckled phrases, in order to allow the pen to then dream a smidgeon.) Spending the day with Alia (and if I omit the dearly burly roles, cello-deep, of her mother in all of this, it is because I write here solely from the eyes of an adoring father) is like surfing a series of waves – a visitor bade welcome to play by the seaside, by the obeisant sea, offering up sacrifices and due honors due. Up and down, round and round, rough and tumble, silken ways, salty skins, sunlight like a tonic. A day at the beach on a holiday that never ends, with choice fare for food offered in the best restaurant in town, for when you might be peckish and wish for a small break from all the fun building castles in the sand and sky. When she laughs, she dances and when she dances her limbs laugh and laugh and laugh. She is the color of merriment in our lives (which now swerves gently into violet, lilac, like the slowly sleeping sun, because she is approaching the longer sojourn of her slumbers.) Alia is joy under a new dispensation, commission. All that's sacred. As she wends her way now to the end of her day, her father enters his rites of mourning. And there is no anthropology for this. Stumped like baffled clowns, pitted with inbound skewing follies, hapless, waylaid, sheer poltroons, these researchers can only pen a doodle. Their words which always hoped to catch the human at the truest turnstile of his being go outfoxed by my darling girl.

The Beach

For Alia

Her first footstep was a stop-start, stop-start;
there was a certain groomed intelligence
about the way she greeted the sand
and the sea's plain before us was nothing

but a feeling, a mood of moving green
in a tapestry of water, the sky a wall
upon which it went, its tale
of wide and horizontal stitch, a promise

of sheer nude adventure,
or like a long flat clock of ticking innocence
by which things might be said and done –
the future's way, not and not and never

a worry for the walking girl.
And by the time the sun began to set,
finding us edited for homeward bound,
she stood up, broke the sand again without a sound,

and walked with me hand in hand
away from the unfinished
business of the sea, away from the lip
of the surf, away and away and away.

And what was most incomplete
about our walk through the sun-kissed day
only arrived at the point of periwinkle night.
Once more, there was a broken thought in sight.

Alia's Alchemy

And there are many ways to spell your name,
because it is a word possessed. And when
it happens to be uttered, it sounds a sound
to solicit the magic of soldered charms;

and the demons who seem to people the air, who
seem to skew the living, no matter where; the demons who
slip through the slits that sunder lovers, even lovers,
like a school of sprites, slotted there between the colors

that drape our bodies, and what we wear
across the flesh – motives, projects, cares –
those demons seem to grow, widen, change,
becoming like better angels for a larger age...

And so, the living turns, pivots crooked to the straighter,
darning with the arts of a newly-naked reign,
where power is like a flourishing, together, and where
the struggle with the gods for the gift of the bitter last

of their godly money, paints a new set of lines
across the skein that paints our lives, that dyes
and dyes again the cloth we wear, as we amble across
our lives... And I cannot gift the sun a face

today, because too much light begs for darkness.
And that your name is enough. It shines from each
and every cell of the skin we own, filler for the breach
between bodies – bound now by its binding of us.

Ad Hominems I

De Profundis

When I walked into the place nothing
happened. I spent a few years
dithering with the sort of thrift you find
peopling giants whose shoulders shuddered
with shaking tears unbeknownst to even
the man who was crying. I tried many things
to assuage and drum against the fears
peopling my skin like crawling insects
whose sprawling bits and pieces stayed intact and just
so. And those were the good years, shall we say,
and those were the years of plenty, the years
when the days were rills. So many ploys since
then played and played again. The immensity
of the inception was staggering and beggaring
and there were eerie truths too like birds
caterwauling and caw-cawing in white
and black like the sky attacked, much as it
was attacked. There was such a glut of
love back then much as there would be later
but then it held itself with a guilty finger and later
guiltier filled with innocence. How deep the scare
back then between the petering colors! How deep
the injustice to himself and to all the others...
These depths find their ending though, in a few coins, in a few rare
coins. And the mint I find still in a ruptured
cheek and a ruptured eye finds its home, its suture
only here: weaves of feeling I cannot count anymore.

A Hunger Artist

After Kafka

All day long he is hungry. The nourishment that he
Hopes for is so large in the distance, and possessed
Of such long and whittled legs, whittling and whittling,
It makes him angry... The righteous and the free
Should not be caged like this, caged and made to pay
This toll, this tax, this fee. As he views the wrongs
He pays himself, the storms of his gift, the stress:
He wonders, as though a note on a passing stave,
About this music, this beat, these feet: he raves
And rants his sum of warning wisdoms, because
He can't forgive the one man who placed him here.
He can't forgive the way this drama of unwinding fear
Plays itself across the stage of his exhibits. The leers
Of the well-fed crowd, milling around, passing by,
Speak in tongues to him he can't quite parse
Or gloss: he's never quite understood what it is
To be a man or woman like this: plain, plain-spoken,
Hanged hungry for the simple things whose utmost token
Is to be satisfied – the length and width of those fat
Fires, needs, slaked for all to see: as he does, too, sadly. The stet-
Like finish they evince, this passing, passing crowd, make him feel
A stranger before an even stranger god. And as he kneels,
Offering up a doubtless waylaid prayer – chaser for the food
At the last, that might prove sturdy and burly and good –
He views again the weirdly filmic scene he's trapped within:
This reel, turning on repeat, burning like the infinite sin
It always was, and is. It was always easier for him to be
Hungrier than the rest, angrier, fearful, worried, unfree:
Because the food made to beat and sate his hunger
Named him, always, in ways he failed to like or love. So, he
Wishes to stay weak like this, frail, farther from the stronger
Ways of a stronger body – which is safe in its safety,
Sure in its sureness, certain of the same old certainties
An artist can never know, feeling all things as they bleed.

Education

Dubai

When the carrion birds peck and squabble,
When they build the amateurs of their essays
Where all the organs of the slain are discussed,
There are always one or two of them who
Think themselves vultures better than the rest,
Who come-off like snobs, because, as they eat,
Still parrying away the others – who are also eating
Down from the sky's fluent freedom the meat
Of the dead – they give themselves these airs.
These uppity few are so proud of their education,
About knowing the things to do in all situations,
The others waiting in the gorging queue
Are put off, strangely, from their bloodied food.
They feel it's unfair. And they seem to resent
The one or two carrion birds who lend
Their bloody, picky work the sheen
And blend of some endeavor of bettering.
They want what they do, animals at the last,
To be known for what it is: no sense of class
Or of classiness should ever be permitted
The look of the work of a good, fast,
Famished carrion bird. The uneasy question
That seems to rumble from their lips – while spilling
The munched-at gruel of dead, flayed meat,
Mixed with the fandangos of a bird's saliva –
Is a question about effrontery. The chutzpah
Of those few birds, the sheer uppity gumption!
Who do they think they are? And how: better?
And in their minds, and in their minds alone
Those who seem, so effortlessly, superior
Are actually the only truly humble birds left
In the annals of this famished tribe. Bereft
Now of the old scholastic cue, the way that birds
Once upon a time knew what they knew,
These few birds of dead attack, so attacked,
Can only keep their silence, faced by major fiat.

Lawrence Durrell

For my uncle, Waddah Faris, who led me there

Picture here a ravenous teen,
His mind, a widening O, a famished mouth,
His throat, dry.

One night, thirsting, parched, lean
From a strangely stoppered south
Through hungering eyes,

A young man strolls to a mahogany shelf
And finds himself a pick, picked-out,
And finds a self

Now in the grip of a self's new brew –
Rendered special, choice, cured
By a magical uncle, maternal, world-toured.

The tome then handed him
Was a white chunk of likely muscle – a watercolor
Across the thickset front

With dripping lines always meant to be
Mysteries, elliptical. English, or French
By way of the language of the first,

It was a book come to stretch and slake
A deep, an ambitious thirst.
Here were words in a sea of words, in a sea unseen –

And the artist behind them,
Beneath them, and through,
Came wrapped inside the glitch

Of a man who excels (can't but)
By way of the flaws that seem, always, to pit
Each newborn artist, each newborn flare, born

A glazing swan, a blade of grass, and then
Blackened, sweetened
By the colored portions of his character –

Prisms, curios, nibbled with arcane spirit.
I'd read through the works of men
And women by then. But this

Proved to be my first true love,
A find and a fund and a founding.
And I was ravenous, raved a rave

Across the face of what now became
A razed tablet. My mind turned, a swiveling sum
Grown larger, newly-bitten, swift to rise

Again, and again, by the shape of words,
The color of new-found words,
And sense behind sense behind sense

In the moving layered depths there, in the mint
Of what looked like a thick white tome
Of pages, and that alone; words in a storm

Of rapt discovery; words in a bluster,
Tearing the heart away, much like money –
But with names that had no names as yet,

Currency for no lit market – only
The quicks and the errancy of a word like this,
Found (with others) by a type of torturous kiss:

Precipice,
      precipice,
            precipice

2. Wishful Thinking

The Spelling Of Our Skies

For Alia

Riven, and made to drift, the troubles
With which in sadness she comes and goes
So equipped, are nothing like a warzone
In the end, or what you might expect
From the telltale of the bones
That love like this, muscles that are metals.

And even if
The big bad blazoning
At hand is naught but a single hand
That may have lost its peer, its second
In a chance of two,

Here's a veering wish —

And even if
It means the flinging
Of a harsher stone between us
Here's a nearing wish
To solve the warring voice, as it travels...

How does one reach a girl from whom
A woman comes and goes; and then, how to
Unfurl the secret of the text: and how
With a humble hermeneutic
Find the clock beneath, traveling, tick-tock-tick?
How find the true center of the room
In a house like this, a house too late, perhaps, too soon?

Simply, I don't know — for all the strident fears
That force me to... But then, as I near

This perfect middle,
This perfect spot in the melee and the muddle
Of two lives and their troubles,
I hone my eyes in hope and lift
My eyes with that same precision

To the horizon of a darling child,
The dearest spelling of our spelt-out skies.

Character

For Alia Sabbagh

First, let her believe in the goodness of things;
From out of the bowl of her heart the burst of a guiltless song.
Let her fall from the hardened garden of hanging lies
Simply because the leaves there are blue, dud, death-dyed.
Let her know truth a truth, her grand iconic points
Those of a star, filigree between the dark blue joints
Of other nightshades. Let her think always
Of light as the only reed to follow, the only gate
Of worth, rank, in a world that may try to try her
With its mist, a darkness seeming closed to surrender.
Let her grip the silver coin of character, smiling grace,
And her fig-hued lips without a wait across her face.
Let her speak well of people, at the last, and even when
They sully her name in the hurried death of a guilty vein.

Defining Self-Respect

To be able to touch your finger against a shadow
And then watch the grey-tilled darkness grow
And grow around the tan and lilac of your skin,
And still to know a thing or two about how to begin
To answer, with a life, or maybe two, life's dun conundrums.

To be able, in short, to offer a piano to a drum,
To watch your hands as they touch the keys
As though they'd violins in their bones, now released.

And when I pose my question about all of this, ask,
Then pressure the dreg of the same blessed question again
To rid myself of shrouds, bar all masked decisions –

It's then, I might reveal the *When* of the bitter rasp
In the voice of the world, as it breaks like a dead leaf
Underfoot: seeming, also, to be asking a thing of love.

A Small Redress Against The Sins Of The Fathers

For Alia

For a short while he lost
his eyes and the finger of the ghost
touched him.

She will sleep a short while and then
play and clap her hands
because girls always do and
like to. So, I listen

for the rhymes in the night trees'
swishing and can only pray
to pay a small price
against the clanging of the night
I pray against

because it would be easier
to take away this
fool's errand of life
than watch my daughter cry
for just a short while for
even that
short while.

The sins of the fathers visit those of us
who are fathers
of daughters who are
fathers
of daughters.

I am younger than she is
of course and the He of God is
stronger in her than He is
in me.

While she sleeps within the thimble
of her dreaming mind
which is larger than vastness
and larger than sweetness
I may say to myself many things
to bring the morning in.

I've lived a long and small life
and a long and smaller
and ask only for this
patterning to bring my daughter
her father back again and if
it comes to it may
God in whatever large strong way
come down into skies
I know.

Hands

For Alia Sabbagh

When she lifts her hands through the lives they lead
as small and white mincing dancers; and then with joy she
offers the rune she knows as first, and primed to be, *One* –
I think of how no final heat, in any final tot or sum
she may ever conjure, dream, will ever be or quite become
the dancing warmth and the dancing love
that comes from these primed digits, the hands that craft
this care – the kind of skill whose art of *Never* is
never enough… Addressed beneath the eaves of this caress,
she wends down from a longer limb than all device
may ever limn or draft or see and touch and size.

Her lilac hands are like good mornings:
they glow inside the girth within
the dawn-sprung gut of morning;
and the whole blue and green load of earth
turns with her dancing hands,
swiveling the air like mystics met by mirth.

Sunlight Upon Sunlight

For Alia Sabbagh

Sometimes, my eyes will catch her caught in her own still moment. It is late afternoon, say, and spears of light angle into the living room, the long deft spears of sunlight almost violet-colored at this waning part of day. My girl might be gamboling in stumbling circles, chasing a fallen or moving toy, or just wandering around in search of the next bit of world to ignite the play of her imagination, the next foil to flame and billow through her like something we adults often recall as joy. And then, just now, there is a moment, a point at which she stops the slipstream of her ambient mind wagging and burgeoning into more and more into life; at which she stoppers the humdrum role or mask of time, corking it, bottling it, only to drink it up the more fluently, presently. She has spied, it seems, a small quadrangle of sunlight reflected or refracted from the partly-shaded, wide wall-wide window, splayed there like a small, rare instance of loyalty or truth upon the Persian carpet – whose rigorous patterns play and dovetail between plum and beige, navy and a rich wheat-grey. The charged citrus shape on the carpet beguiles her. What is there left to do, she seems to think, briefly, but to capture it, grasp it, as though stepping and stepping again on the small, good portion of sunlight were, in a manner, like the learning of a new word. Her greatest wish at this moment, it seems to me, is to reach and demand for the impossible. Likewise, she tries to catch and grip the clouds of smoke, emitted like spirals of mystery, which emerge from my toking mouth; I shouldn't be smoking in her vicinity, of course, but watching her attempt and strive for the impossible is one of the highlights of my day. So, when she steps and steps again upon this shard of sunlight, this workaday presence she makes strange, she is reaching, you might say, for utopia, or a place she's never been to as yet; a place in fact that none of us know; though distantly, perhaps, once a place we looked-to too, searching the illuminate distance.

Chocolate Gifts

For Mohamad and Alia Sabbagh

She is getting cannier now, savvier. Small round pellets, colored
across the rainbow, hold little loads of sweetened chocolate to be
crunched, rolled around the tongue, savored. But there is more to the
sweet gift than this: for it is the cordoned-off domain of only *jiddo's*
care. At first, her grandfather drove the monopoly for self-seeking
reasons, passions; it wasn't meant to be, in truth, an exemplar of the
supposed Marxist 'laws of production', whereby concentration and
centralization of the source of supply are groping, babbling
tendencies one can't resist in a market economy evidenced by the
periodic fall in profits. No: nothing so salacious, tasteless. It was in
fact a quite natural progression in a place as warm and warmed as
this, where power is identical with its better: authority.   No
Gramscian hegemony, achieved by cooption, a surreptitious cahoots-
forming coercion, makes sense here. The hegemon is a father and a
grandfather, and fills these roles without a single stagey mask. The
tenderness as it appears melts all hearts, so that the large wide living
room where this daily rite is performed starts to flow again with rivers
of blood, the oaken wine given time to breathe, mature; the oaken
wine of goodness in the process of being groomed. The chocolate lies
hidden in a cabinet too high for Alia's reach. That said, she now
knows where the stash is, stashed. So, by the third or fourth day
here, staying with my parents, it was not just a case of a grand
surprise in the clenched grip of her *jiddo*; it was, rather, her pacing
forth to tug-at this old and loving man's stone-colored *abaya*, tugging
him at the knees with her right hand while swinging her waylaid left
to point towards the deep mahogany cabinet just round the corner of
her tugging, the while, making small chimp sounds of adorable
appeal The operation of chocolate gifts now has two stages, phases:
two dovetailing parts to what is a darling maneuver. First, the call,
the imperative call from the toddler, wise-to; then, the grand effort
beneath an effortless smile, of rising from the deep seat of the couch,
and goose-stepping for comic relief round to the cabinet.   My
daughter follows my father, amused, but still with a brow's gunning
intent on the prize. Before being gifted a small pellet of sweet, sweet
chocolate, she must name the color in the open hand. She always
does; thus, demand is sated.   And so, this is how the generations
(once again) hook and latch onto each other in the rooting ways of a
family-tree whose soil is love. The sweet gift, the gift of sweets, work
like a chiasmus, thus, whose turnstile between the two opposed
conversions is this smitten middle: father, son.

Playdate

For Alia

When you share your space and toys
And learn to hold your hand, quiet and free
In one single soulful effort
From bad or worser habits, the tics of childish envy –
Dotting, thereby, in comfort your dotty little 'I';

When you stride with that sure precision
The measure of what you own,
A few small paces that turn to the size
Of harbingers, let us say, of a pedigree vision –
Poems to speak your own-most way, your name

Signing its lengthy stay to the finish
Of whatever odd job you later choose
For your précis, your erstwhile sum –
Recall at the last this space, a hope I share
With a seeing poem of simple, easy care;

Remember what it looked like to see
All things from a nearly naked eye,
And recollect the spirit of your father's
Grace through so much time and space
Suffering the blindfolds of others.

Valentine's 2021

For Faten

I want to break through a screen here;
One we've built at deuce, and locked

Inside a strangely flawless battle
Built of fear and fear that's worse
Than that: a harder fear, a hardened
One against the rocks...

So, this is what I want:

To un-shield the utmost truth,
And with a sum of honest breaths
Line my lines like likely minds
While working hard
To disarm them: my only

Weapon will be my honesty.

In short,
I want to land and pierce the broken ice
Of a twofold story, a story, once told twice.

Between the two of us, tied,
Tethered by twofold travesties –
Two mouths, four lips and all and all
That hurts between: I hope to find
The diamond

Inkling, deeply hidden, once again;
Find the glint that gifts the toil
Of scurrying, rummaging hands
Hopes in fertile soils; or just: *the glimmer*

That proves itself, a risen character
Upon this stage; or like a cleansing spirit
Swift to prove itself a peer
To our daunting peerless drama

And all the dirt
We've looked-for – two ravished victims
Busied with the search
For a satisfying sort of failure.

And so, this is all I have to say, as I
Mother words to another mother;

And so, this is what it is today:
Another shot from under cover

At being simple,
So that love might wear again a lover.

The Color Of Blood Becomes Her

For Faten

If I look at you today, a marrow's mauve
Perhaps, or a purple's cotton with the gift
Of red seeping through; if I look and look,
Searching-back to find the searching hook
That had me both: riveted and riven; had me both
The doer of one quick and sure decision
And the maker of a knot; and if I tug, after
Long legs and much hard reading, the length of rope
That makes this war of lengthy hope, surrender:

I see myself as both, predator, provender
In the jungle of our excess; see myself a prowler
Through wilds of eyeless wilderness
In the feral light and feral dark between us,
The softness and the dangers of our daily rote –

And it does in fact become easier to please
The god buried in the blood, or the god
Buried much further in – the chief inside the cells
The flowing blood flows with, making its decisions;

And easier, too, to found if you like, a kind
Of new religion, whereby prayer is clean and pure,
A silent thing one does, and love, a law to be proven
By no one judge – but by the two of us,

Building licit beauty, shall we say, from the mess we might've made,
Farming years of silken fabric out of years of dirt and mud.

The Sacrifice

For Alia

For the lips of my daughter
And what they might come to speak
In time, and what they might say
In words, bolder than the future,

I'm ready to meet each rich sacrifice.

From out of the strange, whole plenty
Given me, staggered by the gift as it
Devolved in staggered shades to this

Small, crammed corner, this shrinking place
Where I'm closer now and close
To being shriven of all in goldenness
That was given – it seems that,

Slotted here on the block,
I've one more last decision to make
For these fig-colored lips, my daughter's.

And later, when, with harsh-voiced questions
They beggar me with the *Why* of it,
And I, less a single cause or coin left
To make a sure reply: I'll simply say
I suffered to be touched with theft
For the redder lips of my daughter.

And then, even later, when they ask
Of my dear lips, and what of mine?

I'll simply say that once upon a time
I had them, but that now there are none.

More

For Faten

You look to a spot that's taken by a star
Because there's so much more
You could be doing,

And so much more, the air above, beneath your
Wings; and more – in lists I cannot bring
To cornicing, polish, finishing.

You've a dark-browed hunger more
Like anger – but possessed, too
At times, of a simpler, lighter hue;

But when the missed ambition strikes
You look at me, busied in my blue
Music, and decide to mar

The day with your temper: tics,
My love, I've gotten used to.

Matter Beyond Matter

For Alia
Dubai

She likes to place words in his mouth
then asks for a kiss to seal them.

The while,
his lips seethe with apple-colored gems
unspoken, fearing, as he does, their new way south
when first she hears them; the innate beauty
of his words, the way they'll now turn, fold,

by the arts of an odd, dark smithy
and spin, tussle with some bad magic in
the air, till they become dun and dross
and all the many things they are not,
the membra disjecta for her many sins,
and all his winnings now painted as loss.

There's no contest here, and there never
was. But those who insist
on competing, with the weapons they know,
with the tools of some learned malice
or mischief, aimed to wound the purest air,
end up even sadder than they ever were…

There's no winner, loser in a life, when true
to itself, and money and sex and power, though
useful at times, run to nothing, or more: to below
nothing in the end. What counts, the number
that matters, is the arced quality of the heart
that went pained, shackled and cuffed
by the one coursing rift that did in fact matter:

what was heard, dressing the air from self to self
when God was in the wings, without a cue,
only listening; only listening, perhaps, to poor old you
turning sky-blue gifts into more sky-blue.

The Neighboring Tribe

Dubai

They live the shape of their lives
formed by the ways of the tribe,
hackneyed, gaunt,
in the slicks and vertigo of their want.

All I want for my daughter
is for the missive in the envelope
of her body to be comprised

by such words that are starlit ways
by which to steer
past the lovelessness in the lie
by which tribe ogles tribe,

covetous, so without hope
of ever meeting the human commission.

And that her message, the one most
deep-set inside of her, might reach her lips

and thereby turn to be
so unlike the muffled motes
she may see and come to know; to be
the kind of person
from whom kindness is not a lesson
or something to be learnt,
but the innate movement that drips

to honey the waters
of the common skein, which is common only

in the way this life is sipped.

Sleep

For Faten and Alia Sabbagh

The walls, buried back by bookshelves,
Seem to drip with the knowledge

That, as much as purple is your favorite color,
There is a seemly time for burrowing
Into your pillow's slowly-steadied earth.

And yet, each night you are a waylaid warrior
Mirrored by the mind's gripped *Now* of a day's long worth –

The sun-steps of the daily pledge
You make, to fight sleep with a clamoring song
That spills in small grandeurs of rising wealth
The sheer wake and measure of you –

And yet, each night you picket the sky
As though it were a tarnished darkness,

Warring your warbles, draped in the fancy-dress
Of a protest, shouting colors at that arc of massive blue,
Because it is unwelcome, an ocean
That wants to hold you down, and to drown you to
Nether regions of nightly naught, unpieced again.

And so, we dare not press the plea
Of timeliness, seemliness, the due and proper cue

To unstrap the wings that may have guided you
Through the day, a wide unvanquished traveler,
Because even here in the seam of sleep

You may need them, once more to see.

Worldliness

For Alia

I suppose some are near-born with it
messing in their blood; and more: and that
there is a kind of cloying, a kind of coveting
beneath the brim of each blood's cell.
I suppose for some life is like a lie
they've never quite escaped from.

There are others, though. They dye
themselves with just as many solecisms,
sure, but what does indeed tell
from out of their passage through the thrum
of living, is the self-awareness in their eyes –
the first note, the last, of their lives' long

while.... And what I wish for my daughter
is for her to greet the world with less of it.
For more, for more wordless laughter.

Letter To An Innocent In A Time Of War

For Alia

You wake each morning to a world
That loves you: four eyes that seem to unfurl
Beneath their bedding lashes, four lives.

And we love you, we do. And our love behaves,
If you like, in a way that no science, that no
Gauge in a measuring gambit, can ever pin or know.

And while the world we live in is filled
With just such innocence, other eyes
And other lives, spread upon the lock

Love is – still, there's a gasp we feel, a shock
To the way we try and try again,
Against all the sour logic of the brittle clock,

To love you. Men and women, just like us, rise
Into being just like this: like lives due to the risen
Truth of one like you, a straight line whose sign's a rune

Spelt past all the myths of our claimed decisions.
We're mad for you, you might say; and from our straightjackets
We'll babble of your innocence with crazed, lit tongues.

Meanwhile, my love, the world's aflame – as the world forgets,
Once again, to douse what has always burned here: blood-red ringed
By more. But you are Jerusalem for us. Less the sadness,
                                    the millennia of sins.

Diplomacy

For Faten

He approaches her, his mouth's softest touch –
But the words are like a beeline, still, sourced
In the glut and cusp of what just must be.

And his lines of approach are like fingers
To caress her skin, a kind of modal poetry
By which the poor in spirit turn to rich –

Founded as much as funded to be found.

And so, the battlefield proves a famished, finished ground

And all the slain: discussed by history
Now the weapons of war have softened
By way of the touch of the blood they've spilled.

It's like the future's a message that none were killed
In fairest combat – a just maul and tiff and tussle.

It's like the past's a missive
Whose envelope
Goes missing, happy to vanish, happy to free
The print within, the words of vivid, penning hope.

From out of the arcs of much fraught narrative,
Peacefully, love's last stand's the ember, alive

In this grate at deuce: approaching or
                                        arrived.

Ad Hominems II

Good Advice

If it's peace you want, the man said,
Be a bough, be a leaf, find their runes and read
In green breaths their green relief. If it's peace
You seek in some final hall of columned grace,

Learn the better and learn the more
Mediocre mores and, face to face
With a simple heart, with a simple mind,
Shear away, much like they do, the simple sin
Of a silken man, of a silken man being svelte
In a plain world planed by what
Only the cloth wants. And the man never

Spoke his name, and the man was like a river
Running through me for many days
After this. He seemed wise,
Building things, forming things from the inside
To the inside. And it was like
He'd no need of any place, and not a need
For any name, nor a name to suit the face

Of a man I saw only once in my life,
And it was a meeting that set the tone
Of all my cleverness from then on.

A Glass Of Water

Dubai

There is something about this man
that makes what it is that's on
the cusp of happening
timely as the tide of what has been.
It's frightful to know the future
as well as this; what was meant to be
a razed tablet comes in the shape
of a cage, tall and sure
and as though to the measure
of some Mosaic law. It's not surprising
to feel the floor beneath your feet beat
to the same sad tune heard before
in the mind of a man with no, with
no memory anymore.

And though the melodic line
is piece and part of a hackneyed vein,
blue beyond blue and blue,
there are still a batch of things this man
wants to understand. How was it
such a mass of workaday people went
gulled and guyed by a fabulous secret
without a window like this? And how,
fooled by the way things might have been?
How is it they agreed to join in dream
like this, droplets in the glamor
of a glass of water it's sure
none would ever have agreed
to sip themselves?

And then, what of the water itself?
It sees of course, hears, goes
touched at the lips, but without a scent.
But when has water ever talked?

When, spoken of the things
that have stalked its clarity,
coloring its whiteness
or lack thereof? And if not,
dyeing its wide largesse, the emptiness,
with the slur of some storm
of starless darkness?

It's strange to see a score like this.
Nil, nil, of course, as it ever was,
the staves denuded.

And strolling along the staggered lines
of this book of sad and elastic music
the black marks seam
in such a way
they disappear
in the weave of what was meant by
the composer.

Skim-Reading

Dubai

Decades on,
The same damned
And darning finger here, touched
As much as touching-at the keys,

Proves to be like a finger
That's slow, that can't quite place its own
Golem of a finger
(So as to be finger within finger)

On what it is that's supposed to be
The god of what has been,
The bringer of the passing years, the stoppered flow
That was water readied to be drunk –
But water, in the end, whose ice was smoke.

No one ever told me. No one ever

Stoked their courage, widened the width
And grace, in now-slowing haste,
Of this slick of pain, above and plain
Upon the face of that horizon
Whose clouds of what might have been

Threw rain and hail, and scarred the land
Which was the walking moving skin
Of a rained-on, of a rained-on man.
I'm certain

That in the fatness of major fiat,
Whatever's meant to be

Touched like the future, that old and creaky reel
Spinning on repeat,

Will be a finger and a pin
Pointing, pointed and complete,
And that the map
Of the chief, the topoi of the skein
Will lead to home, a smile I've known;

And that, with the stature
Of the world in the palm of his hand,
The great cartographer
We all know and love, cherish, fear,

Will write the tome
He always meant to write, and that those
Of us who've not the time, nor the chance,
Nor the gift of the opened sky,
Will have to read the book of their own dear lives

In that cheeky way, ad hoc,
Of skimming through the index.

I'd have liked to be the scholar
That I might have been, rooting through
A dozen libraries

For the one, single, soulful word
I was supposed to know.

The Record Straight

For my family

The blessing was to have been known and loved
by those who've loved and known me.

And if tomorrow my sin-colored skin goes dyed
for the last time, the large blessing's burst
will have been the burst of the due, proper colors.

And what I may have to leave behind may be
one of many telling things: the avid, aching thirst
for knowledge

will be, no doubt, the first deft trait to echo
through the layers of this telling night;

the beauty of my eyes and the beauty
of what those eyes have seen – those too
may prove to be things just short, just shy
of staple human failure. But most of all,

the genius of my living passage will fall
on no deaf ears, and no dumb mouths –

filled by the tilt of the overflowing cup
of the northern intelligence
of those who've loved and known me.

And if I've one sole berth for licit pride,
it was the way I tried to dock with virtue:
it was that, in all truth, that kept me alive.

The good die young. And those who've been not
as blisteringly good as they were always meant
to be: die younger – but blessed by the scent

they follow into death. It's a cruel thing
to be cheated of your due – the ring finger,
shall we say, missing the roundest of rings.

3. Broken Thoughts

The Paradox

Dubai

Imagine a woman of deep-set culture.
And right at the telling center
Of her expertise,

Right at the exact point where
The taut string of her well-primed bow
Sets the arrow

On its destined path, released
For the point of purposed murder –

I, a man with two good eyes,
Finds himself, diagnosed,
A poser, perhaps, yes,
But one, I'd hope, not quite equal to the lies

That are posed to him.
Is it a guilty finger pointing, perhaps?
Or, telltale, some deep sin?

A Friend

Through a slit, you lie,
the nook and cranny of your significance.
You like to take a stand on air
and often, the direction of your words
from the deep bruised angle
of your plum, your plummeting surds,
goes nowhere, the sooner abysms
you speak, silly to the point of lullaby,
mouthing tunes, making melodies
towards sleep's good lips.

And while you remain a friend
in faith to your own dear pride,
the bottom of that bond (forged
with such brave and null excess)
will fall beneath the spot you place
your feet upon. In fact,
the beckoning of the ground,
that earthing where each of us is found
for their ambient silver,
is a law of nature, it seems,
you cannot find
between the pages of your science.

The Specialist

Dubai

She has this special gift, a watcher of souls.
And it looks as if she carries them, filled
With the load of their bad boasts, across the river
That's as black as their hearts, these
Dead men and women,
And as viscous, and as syrupy
As the lives they led – and all agree
They were lives that lacked, lives that were
Quicker, too, at skirting past, and sneakily,
And with a school of utmost shimmies
The badness of their course. The fools,
In short, who got waylaid. Errancies, solecisms.

And as she comes to use
The arts of her dark skillset,
Helping the dead across, men and women
Whose wills have turned to broken numbers,
She seems to flow, in her element,
Like another river within
The wider river she helps them with.

They, the wicked dead, pass
But are tutored, too, by a second travesty
And one that lasts; the boatwoman,
And all agree, who drives, and is driven by
This, her specialism,
A skill of pure and pointless space placed
In hell there: well, *she is a specialist*
Whose one loud moneyed yell
Seeks destruction – killing the souls of those
Already bound for hell
A second time. But more than this,
And deeper, and more profound –

Even the god beneath the world
Whose grip in the worldly balance
Was always steady
Regrets the dame and this, her place

In the new economy
                    of infernal things.

The Authoritarian Personality

She spends her days and spends her years
Wrapped in wonder. How is it,
She seems to ask, but without saying it pat,

There are persons whose freedom
To think or roam are gifts, gone pleated so
Well inside themselves, watering each and every hollow,

And how is it, more, that for her it is a fear
To think it – *liberty*: pillow among powers,
And a supposition to be searched?

Is this how a valley, low, damp, dreams?
Is this the way the taller mountains come to tempt
People like this to break their seams and burn

The church of what's been taught them,
Told them? What is there to learn here
But the way that some people hurt?

No Two People

I see it in her eyes, the way those downcast daggers
arrive, only to register where blade hits on blade.
And there are others, too, I know who've seen it:
this globular, sodden look, with wetness without wet.
No two people were ever here. And if the heart's
anything left to say, and say with the same guileless art,
it's that no two people were ever here. She's made
her bed now, as I've made mine, two sottish errors,
let's say, too quick in the cloth of the sheets. And her
face, unveiled now for what it is, is somehow neater –
but like a shroud from the mask she was wont to build:
somehow cleaner for the skin's sheer finish. I never knew
there were so many people living there and yet, so few.

The Manichee

Beneath the noonday sun, you fight
with your shadow: it's a foretold gambit.
To the question of who, exactly, you are,
you fight back with you, a riven answer.

And it's not just a token of brave dehiscence
I see; it's the inborn, the innate manner
by which the perfect splits your temper,
as it tries its essays of little sense...

Sometimes, you will fly-off, a long way gone,
to enter territories – all the viscid wrongs
done to you; and on those lands of hurt
the sickle, the scythe, must do their work.

But there is another part of you, another
part, like another section of the book
whose fluttering pages, baffled by dog-eared
looks, speak of your rising – speak and speak

as well of the sheer mad effort it took
to latch like others onto the light
of being friends in faith with your own
dear self... And so now, in the corner

of your finishing, the way the polish
proffers a sheen that's as you'd wish,
your meaning's the golem or the incubus
of the troubles you've so deftly crossed –

like a wanderer into life, or like a thought
that finds its berth in a waiting mind.
And it's the dock I've always wished for:
where my own small boat of life

finds itself at anchor, me and all
the native peoples of my white...
And it's by the lullaby, by the tuneful
music, they dance, these peoples,

making excellent rhythms out of love…
But then again, for all this, for all this
ratcheting at the last, for all this
finished form from out of shattered glass,

you stay split between the perfect water,
a river's clean stream, cosseting a daughter
of magnificence, and the darkest laughter
catching you, once upon a time, perhaps, forever after.

A Gentleman

And if you're run-through with weakness
You are clean-run through. And even if
The whole of your address apes at love,
It is only hate, a vileness, I know, you live by.

You were never, not like the rest of us,
Meant to die, and in dying learn of flight
Or of a voice as it trembles upon the air,
Teetering between a warble and a war.

And if you're speared by all your weakness,
Your body a pierced and unloved place,
Perhaps you might think again
Of what it is to be a woman. A man

Can bow his head, and play trusted, fair,
But sooner or later, the kind of fluent care
He looks-for he sees – but here, no longer…
A woman may write with a woman's good letters,

But, my dear, the alphabet's the same, and in
The same darning, forming tongue, the man
In this taut tangle, finds it simpler to name
What he sees in runes that bear no fame

Between the walls of your common sense…
But then, it remains a still and pleasant
Evening, and I don't wish to be
Anything but a gentleman.

A Woman's Dialogue With Herself

You might say ambitious strides make a woman strong
And that she'll do her best there to commandeer
The respect that she deserves. I, by turns, prefer the more
Oaken ways of certain sturdy bliss; a sureness that walks
Quietly, knowing the silent paths by which silence speaks
From a clean-run heart. Then, draped with dust and dun –
A daft and waylaid moment, the kind of timeless error
At times we all commit – a woman commands the woman again.
But there are more than two sides to any doubled song,
But there is one, that is to say, and there is only one.
We all opine, of course, bearing fears that feed the same.
We all have views of things, and all of us, our own good names
To protect against wrong. A problem alights, however, only when
You defend yourself from the attack of the self you now disown.

The Diary Of A 'Loser'

For Alia Sabbagh

I want to teach my daughter how to win in life.
This will need some work. She must grow
First, and in the real and more than one sense,
To understand the things her father's learnt
Over many hard years, lost to life's dissent.

That when you gift the world around you
The gifts your kindness owns, not sparing in the coin
Through which you taught yourself

And without a finger taxing tax across your many-fingered shelves

To be taught by ore,
The ore found best inside yourself
When the last wing you ever owned was cut,

And when you have everything a girl could want,
And when the livid, stark catastrophes
Happen into life, as they no doubt will,
And even when your life is thieved, brazenly as it will,
And over many hard and burning years –

That you hold your grip through brittleness,
The lie a life can turn, that you whiten the lack in things
With a smile, having grace, bold only in the needed case.
That you honor even those who've lost

The last shred of decency on the same sea tossed.

That you hold your own in a quiet way,
Showing people, the people all about
You the secret they do always keep,

Knowing in their hearts where they've lost
Without knowing how to show it, not knowing
How to let the small and winning light
You may have shown them in,
Not knowing even that it *was* such, such light that
Made them feel the hint of some distant shame
When they bickered and dared in the grappling there,
Puzzled by how it was you kept your head
Like a widow, or like a widower
Above the many deaths spelt and told you,

And the wife that life becomes, wanting nothing

But to know the how of it, then comprehend
The achievement in her face, how you lost
And won against the long sad history of them,
The long sad history
Which was nothing like money, or the money in your name,
Or even the courage of love. How it was

Merely you
Being honest, and as honest as you could, and as good,
When all the life that life ever knew
From all her winnings won within
Was the confidence of none.

How it was you felt it too
When she spoke again of losing
And you a father, clearly, to all of loss.

The Lay Of The Land

'Home is so sad...'
      Philip Larkin, 'Home is so Sad'

Look at the way the land curves here,
Undulant in parts, fluid and like water,
But holding, too, these dim and tiny crevices
Where a sure foot may slip and then desist
From being what it was, one sure foot of two.
Look at these smallish plots I try not to use
For ground; and how my head and mind, the while, stay
Above it – *and that*, for however long they may...
Look at the ways of this strange cartographer:
She maps it all and for all to see; all, that is, except for her.

Broken Thought

'I look. You look
Away...'
                R.S. Thomas, 'All Right'

I see the wind's manner, its elegant reach
Through leaves, rustling them in their seat
Of pleasant air; you see
The same wonderful movement, the eloquence
Of air, but hurried, and, hurried, sent
Like an invisible scourge.

I cannot stay here long enough to teach
You the ways of thought
As it sits on air, empty
But for the barest wonder, bound with the sense
Of the actual in nakedness... *Yes*, I meant
To teach it you, but now the urge

For that has flown. A broken home's
A place for nothing to be thought, nothing to be known.

Cage

When these bars show-off their industry,
Cogs of a cage, machine;
And then, slotted in this trap, when
I try to show my own way free

Of the fault-lines in the character
Of one who likes to speak of love
With so much industry, a stoppered girl
Still, speaking from a perfect rib

Or one she thinks her redder heart rubs
Against or with, beating its ready whirl
Across the stark imaginary of
A girl; and when – with her open slur

Of trying ownership, a lock, or jealousy –
I pitch my arrows to a better, hoped-for air
Between us: perhaps the wound inside
The grinding of this dull machine may find

Her way through to earth at last,
Digging and chugging till all this noise
Turns to some kind of fathomed gold –
The deuced music of two getting younger, old.

The Plagiarist: A True Story

Dubai

'... *a passing stranger on the road to grief...*'
            John Burnside, 'The Good Neighbour'

I know a man, a man I've come to know,
and he tells me scores of tidbits that seem to grow
in interest the more he speaks of them to me.

He colors each and every tale, *and verily*, he makes one see
between the boughs and between the sparring leaves
the very essence of what it means to be a man like me...

In many wooden minds that ape and strive – groping
like smallish hirsute beasts at that liberty that belongs
to the close-braced discipline that sings in song –

you find their strides grip at the patent barking loss alone
of dwelling, turning wide of any passing route, rootless
all along. *And it's then* this man, a merely passing friend,

learns again a certain openness, true of all true tales:
it's then he learns the ways of men, such binding women,
children in a kiddy play, lost in a game they've never glossed,

gone busied by the scopes of things they fear and cannot tell.
And with that knowledge my friend cuts just one more notch
upon the deadened walls of his ersatz hell – forged to catch

him between the rocks. But he makes no mistakes, doing well;
and turns to the marked-up walls and to the penned-on people,
and tells them again the kinds of thing in kindness he's been told.

Inconsolable

She's this tic. But she's rarely inconsolable.
She holds all the bits of broken glass
In her hands, and holds them so they may last
To cut again the other hands she'd like to lull
To a different state to hers of *Unbeknownst*.

She grips the grey-white shards, wishing with the cuts
And, turning in desperate cycles of disgust,
Her lover finds instead of love the dance
Of a crazed, righteous anger. So, he bids goodbye
To the house of glass she's built, to the evil

Way of one bereft a coin to her shamming hands,
Not a coin, at last, a beggar even might ever stand
To plead for… And it's not the long list of lies,
The millionfold manners of deceit, and it's
Not the deep-set fault-lines there for all to see,

Which shake then shatter the ground beneath
Their feet; it's far simpler than that. It's the shame
His eyes now know, the sanity of the irises
Turned a pupil's black, tutored by a shroud.
He chose this. He chose disconsolation.

In a starlit sky, in which all the signs
Were present and lit with a feral light,
He chose this; he chose to see alone the night's
Dark blue, and not what his soul-filled sanity knew.
That the loveless welcome only lovelessness.

The Criminal

This is my favorite light. And in all honesty now –
Feeling like a piece of this soldered, melting light
Where beige meets lit grey, warmed stone –
It's time at last to say whom I think you are:

You are like a dark sky whose depths of night
Seem to unravel backwards, like navy mountains
Finding, in their darkly rolling furtherance, the care
They never held and never knew pass away

Once again. You are a maze to yourself, a maze
Without point as yet or center. All we do,
Those of us who know you, is try to show you how
A labyrinth like this will only madden you

Into just one more heat, wave upon wave,
The fathomless tides that drive you, moonless
But readied for the way that gravity behaves –
Even if, as all know well, it's a law you can't obey.

Portrait Of A Man

Beirut

The artist we seek may be a master gone missing;
His small blue sign occludes, a blunt mark from a blunt-used
Tool. So, all we have is the painting, left here like a draft
Of where perhaps in time and place a man had loved
In the lineaments of a lived, felt age, facing us.

And when the scholars, as they must, do their digging,
Trying to historicize what just must have been,
Searching for the man (or perhaps, the woman)
Who painted this image, a felled angel formed like this,
Who dealt in the fabric of a seeming saint,
Who'd felt, it's clear, the presence of a certain native goodness
Like silk, a suggestion, upwards, outwards from the paint,

The record, after long and muddy work, shows
Nothing. And all suppose it was a weakness in the painted man,
Questioned and scored by lines of paint as they went
Duly into figured dream, colors mounting colors as if
To burden the picture's frame with the touch of rapt dissent
As it hangs there on the wall, curated like a dare

To posterity. And none, I think, will ever
Unwrap the mystery of this painted face, more
Like a tone of voice, a kind of forlorn music, slowed;
And none will ever be daft enough to look to the far
Corner of the image, a point almost painted-out.

There, we must assume, a wound resides—some unhappy woman
Going on to lie; devising, like only a worn, hurt woman can,
While petering the face we see with the horror of its vision
There at the corner of some fogged or failed decision.

And the painter's question seems to catch him here,
This man of so much strength, and of so much fear,

Only at the moment of his own sheer excision.

The Poisoned Tip

When you are like most, like all, and live
Pinioned against the wall,
Tethered, tied, for the execution of it all;

When a lover, thus, lives the love
Of her erotic attack, deep and swerving,
Voluptuous, passional;

When a man comes to know the full
Purport of a girl, the grace and wound
A woman always brings—

The mouth of a body's passage without sound
Through gauntlets that are like prisons
In which she mirrors pain with pain—

Perhaps then, sane or not, he may holler
And shriek, his skull
Chewing the upstart of his erstwhile soul,

Learning again the poisoned tip that errs
Through air, hurtling after hurt,
As it aims to siege and pierce the fort,
                              a breastbone.

Orientalism,

Or,
Method And Intention

Beirut

My wife is a good Lebanese:
She spends her days searching for the purple
Oriental imagery,

The high-flown and loose and deep
Hydra-headed keep
In which the east's its canny hoard –

Wings and dolls
Found in a treasure-box of words
I'll never understand.

The while,
It's English that's my possession
Here, as I'm quietly possessed, then

Transmogrified like a myth,
Or like the ways a myth
Seems to gloss a human truth.

Simpletons, you see, are furlongs far
From simple: and it's a limpid simpleness
For which I reach, unmarred.

And so, beneath the broken bricks,
The sad mouth's smear,
I try for good, pure English. *And then it nears*

This dwelling-place
Where my good, small part of time, space,
Homes, a honing force,

A kind of magnetism:
And I'm the driven insect
Here returning to its source.

112

Unhomely

Dubai

Another morning at the front.
The quiet is nothing like quiet.
The trenches we've dug are new again,
though they've been there, too,
like rat-colored lines
in sludge for most of the war
to date. In most wars, in even those
that are not in any way salient,
the sparring parties are wont to give
to each other the gifts
of an enemy's parting respect.
But when the enemy grows like rot
inside your boot and your foot
turns from tan to green,
bloodied by the way you start to pick
at it, it's then you might
realize the fight's
slicker than you ever knew.
The barbed wire's a sinch
compared to this; and even when
it cuts and cuts and cuts you
with its ghastly unruly
curlicues of twisted metal
at the least you see
the turning of the blades
that may mark your finish.
To love a woman might be like this,
to see and know your finish
for what it is. But I've no such luck.
She is infinitesimal, close
to invisible
as the last hour loses itself
inside its liminal
last moment
and you, alone for your passage
to the other side and to
a new home.

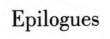

Epilogues

The Silent Oryx

For Maha Faris Sabbagh, on her birthday

In a small, warm corner of this place
A bunch of mint ascends, wafts like wraiths and glowing embers

Neither green nor white; they're like a baffled, unknown race
Of lovers in graceful carousels who serenade the mute and naked air;

And in the small, warm silence it makes amends
For all that made much and so little sense. That said, though,

Your mothering was a flame of a stamp that was always so
Mysterious, smoke in the bones of your emerald gaze...

It is autumn now. And now in the autumn of your days
May the coming of winter be and be and be, happy, capricious –

Some girlish, twirling summer dress
Beneath the beelines and the golden emanations;

Some girlish warmth, let's say; and – salmon-thick – a smile that may
Confess the Care was worth it, building children, burning nations.

80 In The Frame

For Mohamad Sabbagh, on his 80ᵗʰ birthday

The gravel-colored stubble holds no hint of vulture-
Grey, laid with dovish breath (a coat to the raw pink filet
Your skin evinces) sat or splayed – a sage there –
Before the thrilling grammar old age receives, a flickering TV.
The den in which you recline at times – which is a door
Onto gripping worlds offering no slowness or dissent
Or bitterness, or rancor – that was always your space
For idleness and pleasure, shade without shadow.

But now, in the calm browned light of you, your
Weighted age, coffee-colored, wise, and with eighty years
As the background to your foreground –
Perhaps we might discern again the frame within
This well-framed picture, a drawing drawing-out
The truth drawn-in: and the window of a certain melody.

Twenty Years In The Making

If I look back through the tunnel of twenty years,
I see this boy, graceful, and more: fueled by a weird
Desire to be graceful; and yet, I can count the fears
Possessing him, a string on an abacus whose beads
Addle and grin like the simplest numbers: far less
Than what he might have wished-for, and more
Like the way that wish was pressed, all unrest,
With the sense of a muffled, of a broken need.

And here he is again, a whittled number now
Held in sight of a whittled eye. And below
The surface of twenty years: the far deeper show –
A sort of beast disclosed, revealed by a human sound.
It's so darned long ago. And long ago, when love
Was a round corner he grappled with, the long *If*
Young men greet in so many different ways.
Twenty years are flown. And twenty years that stay.

And perhaps the way the years have fallen
Are no one's fault, but mine. But to begin the effort
To uncoil the spring, to unlock the bone-sad bales
And sheaves of meaning, is a project for a different man,
Older, younger – who can tell? For the harvest of these
Passing years goes summed in two stark ways: I survived
A human terror – but lived beneath the tenor of what was
Always meant for me. And any winnings through it all

Are like twenty and like ten: two different numbers
Speaking to each other across a wind-picked valley.
So many things I wished for, things set deep in me,
Things for which I built, as best I could, my fort
Of life, have been split and sundered from my mind.
But I look back across the rough topography of twenty
Years, feel my feet whisper across the hard-pressed turf,
And think that, for all that, I've been luckier than most.

Omar Sabbagh is a widely published poet, writer and critic. His first collection and his fourth collection are, respectively: *My Only Ever Oedipal Complaint* and *To The Middle of Love* (Cinnamon Press, 2010/17). His 5th collection, *But It Was An Important Failure*, was published with Cinnamon Press near the start of 2020. His Beirut novella, *Via Negativa: A Parable of Exile*, was published with Liquorice Fish Books in March 2016; and he has published much short fiction, some of it prize-winning. A study of the oeuvre of Professor Fiona Sampson, *Reading Fiona Sampson: A Study in Contemporary Poetry and Poetics*, was published with Anthem Press in July 2020. A paperback, revised edition of this work was published in late 2021. His Dubai novella, *Minutes from the Miracle City* was published with Fairlight Books in July 2019. He has published scholarly essays on George Eliot, Ford Madox Ford, G.K. Chesterton, Henry Miller, Lawrence Durrell, Joseph Conrad, Lytton Strachey, T.S. Eliot, Basil Bunting, Hilaire Belloc, George Steiner, and others; as well as on many contemporary poets. Many of these works are collated in, *To My Mind Or Kinbotes: Essays on Literature*, published with Whisk(e)y Tit in January 2021. Presently, he is working on a Lebanese verse novel: *The Cedar Never Dies*. He holds a BA in PPE from Oxford; three MA's, all from the University of London, in English Literature, Creative and Life Writing, and Philosophy; and a PhD in English Literature from KCL. He was Visiting Assistant Professor of English and Creative Writing at the American University of Beirut (AUB), from 2011-2013. Currently, he teaches at the American University in Dubai (AUD), where he is Associate Professor of English.